THE

PURPLE

MARTIN

BY

R.B. LAYTON

NB

NATURE BOOKS PUBLISHERS

First Printing	1969
Second Printing	1970
Third Printing	1971
Fourth Printing	1972

Price: $3.98

Mailing address:

NATURE BOOKS PUBLISHERS
Post Office Box 12157
Jackson, Mississippi

Library of Congress Catalogue
Card Number 71–92883

International Standard Book
Number 0–912542–01–2

Printed in the United States of America

THE PURPLE MARTIN
(MALE AND FEMALE)

COVER PHOTOGRAPH COURTESY S.A. GRIMES,
JACKSONVILLE , FLA.)

iii

MALE RELAXES
ABOVE THE DOORWAY

TOO MANY FOR
ACCOMMODATIONS

iv

THE PURPLE MARTIN, *Progne subis*

FAMILY — Swallows (*Hirundinidae*)

LENGTH — seven to eight inches

DISTINGUISHING FEATURES — *Male* is glossy black or violet, with purple iridescence (wings and tail a duller black than head and back).

Female is light breasted in contrast to male. Easily distinguished by gray color on its breast (male's breast is dark like remainder of body).

Both have long wings and moderately forked tail.

RANGE — Peculiar to the Americas. Breeds west of the Cascade Range and Sierra Neveda mountains of California from southwestern British Columbia south to Baja California, northwestern Mexico (Sonora) and Arizona. East of the Rocky Mountains it breeds from eastern British Columbia, across southern Canada to Nova Scotia and to the Gulf Coast and southern Florida (and in the West Indies). The winter range is primarily in South America.

EGGS — White and unmarked, with an average size of 1″ x 3/4″.

NEST — Constructed mainly of grass, straw, twigs, and mud. Located in tree cavities, holes in cliffs, and in man-made houses. Martins are gregarious, always nest in colonies.

FOOD – Flying insects (bees, mosquitoes, flies, beetles, moths, dragonflies).

COLOR VARIATION – Purple Martins from the southwestern deserts of North America tend to be smaller and lighter in color than those elsewhere. This interesting adaptational feature presumably allows for greater reflection of the desert heat.

CONTENTS

PREFATORY REMARKS

This little book is primarily for the layman. In it he will find the most interesting and essential information about the life and habits of one of America's most attractive birds. This study is based upon years of observation of the martin by the author, as well as upon numerous reports of other martin fanciers, naturalists, and ornithologists. The remainder of the information about the Purple Martin, which completes the picture, is included here simply because it is extremely fascinating (reason enough!) —— the mystery of the martin's migration, what it eats, how it nests and raises young, how it fights . . . I have thought it best to illustrate the book generously with photographs and drawings, for such vivid pictorial records about the martin lend a great deal to the narrative of description.

The book is in fact a product of observation, both by myself and others. Some of the information has been published before (mostly in obscure scholarly publications), some has not. For use of data which was collected and published by others, I am deeply grateful. As it seemed best not to burden the text of a book of this sort with technical footnotes, I have mentioned my principal debts in the Bibliography and tried to indicate there the nature and value to me of the articles and books which I consulted. These provide a basis for further study of the Purple Martin which the reader may wish to undertake.

At this point, however, I must record my thanks to several persons, both professional scientists and laymen, for sharing with me their insights through personal communications and through correspondence. Chief among these is Professor George H. Lowery, Jr., of Louisiana State University; also Professor William E. Southern of Northern Illinois University; Professor Edwin Franks of Western Illinois University; Mr. Earl B. Baysinger of the United States Fish and Wildlife Service; Mr. R. J. Landis, Mr. Pearl Bourdine, Mr. Lester Alvis, and Mr. Samuel A. Grimes.

For excellent photographs I am indebted to Mr. Samuel A. Grimes, the Humble Oil and Refining Company, and others for whom courtesy lines are shown.

Also to my son, who kindly read the typescript and made some suggestions in matters of style. But I save until the end to mention the deep gratitude I feel towards my wife — who offered so much support and help in the production of the whole manuscript in general—(and of design in particular)——and remember with pleasure the many hours and miles of travel in search of information and photographs and the many hours spent together in the backyard patio watching the Purple Martin, whose life is described in the pages and pictures of this book.

FEMALE LISTENS TO MALE IN APARTMENT SELECTION

TWO FEMALES CONFER

A NORTH AMERICAN FAVORITE

"One swallow doesn't make a summer," but one Purple Martin does mean that spring is almost here.

The Purple Martin, largest of the swallow family, has been a favorite in North America for many generations. And rightly so, for hardly any other bird can be so truly called an American as our cheerful little friend *Progne subis*.* Its migratory range is extensive, and in the spring and summer the martin inhabits all the United States and southern Canada, from coast to coast. More daring members of the family are often spotted as far north as the Vancouver Islands and southern Saskatchewan, while a few hardy ones even range beyond, to Cape Prince of Wales, Alaska, only 75 miles from the Arctic Circle!

---

*This nomenclature for the Purple Martin, in international use by zoologists, follows the system of the great Swedish biologist Carl von Linne, or in latinized form,CarolusLinnaeus, after whom it is called the *Linnaean system:* Linne (1707-1778) published his nomenclature system in a work called *Systema Naturae* (1758).

The Purple Martin's arrival in the spring is welcomed by young and old alike, just as its autumnal departure can be a source of deep regret. But migrate it must, to satisfy some mysterious urge that modern science yet has not explained to the fullest. With its annual trips between North America and South America, it lives almost its entire life in the air, exceeded in this respect perhaps only by the swifts, smaller swallowlike birds that breed in chimneys and never perch on wires or twigs. The martin is one of the few birds that is seldom seen on the ground. It catches its food on the wing, drinks water by dipping down into ponds and lakes and raises its young in selected sites above the ground. In fact, almost the only time that it can be seen on the ground is in search of twigs and other nesting materials during the nesting season.

The martin is outstandingly gregarious — no self-respecting martin would consider living alone — and this desire to socialize with its fellows is matched only by a willingness to live in the midst of human civilization, in practically every type of bird house imaginable.

ARRIVAL IN SPRING

The Purple Martin's annual spring arrival in the United States takes place during that period which extends from late January through April. Within this period, the arrival date for any one locality can be quite regular, so that a given observer may find that it does not vary more than an interval of two to four weeks. It is surprising how punctual our little friend can be! For example, I have logged martin arrivals at my own colony over a period of several years and noted a fluctuation of only about twenty days (between February 26 and March 16). They do not arrive on the same day, year after year.

The vanguard of these welcomed spring and summer residents makes its way across the Gulf of Mexico from South America and up the Yucatan Peninsula, to spread across the United States and finally into Canada. Studies show that the Purple Martin also breeds in Lower California (Baja California) and northwestern Mexico, as

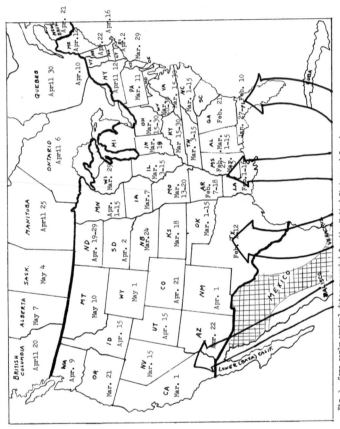

Fig. 1   Some early arrival dates recorded for the United States and Canada
Cross hatched area ⧉ indicates nesting range in Mexico

well as on the central plateau at least as far south as Jalisco and Veracruz (see figure 1). But on the other hand, very few records show the Purple Martin to be an inhabitant of Central America.

As we move further south, we soon come to the area to which the martin returns after a summer in North America (figure 2). Evidence for the Purple Martin's South American range has been revealed only recently as wintering in northern, eastern, and southeastern Brazil, with a high concentration presumably within the Amazon Basin. To some extent the martin inhabits all the northern countries of South America and adjoining islands (Trinidad and Curacao) as well as the east Andes region from Colombia to Bolivia.

Figure 1 is a map giving the earliest arrival dates of the martin for all states of the United States and for the southern provinces of Canada. Using this map, it is possible to obtain some idea of when to expect the Purple Martin in one's own area. Remember that these are early arrival

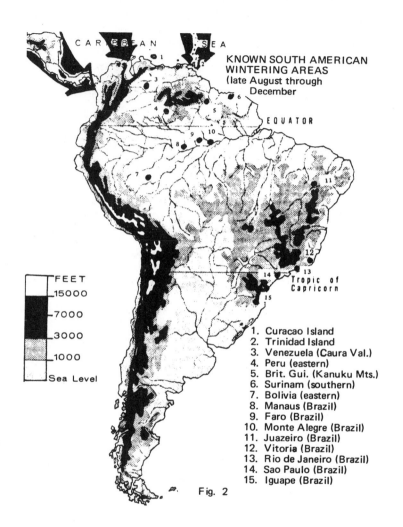

KNOWN SOUTH AMERICAN
WINTERING AREAS
(late August through
December

1. Curacao Island
2. Trinidad Island
3. Venezuela (Caura Val.)
4. Peru (eastern)
5. Brit. Gui. (Kanuku Mts.)
6. Surinam (southern)
7. Bolivia (eastern)
8. Manaus (Brazil)
9. Faro (Brazil)
10. Monte Alegre (Brazil)
11. Juazeiro (Brazil)
12. Vitoria (Brazil)
13. Rio de Janeiro (Brazil)
14. Sao Paulo (Brazil)
15. Iguape (Brazil)

Fig. 2

FEET
15000
7000
3000
1000
Sea Level

dates, recorded by someone in each state. We wish to point out here that the Purple Martin frequents mountain areas much less than the remainder of the area, particularly is this true in the arid Rocky Mountain range.

The northward movement of the martin takes place at a rather leisurely pace and for many areas is yet not fully understood. In South Carolina, for example, their arrival has been recorded from February 7-16, while in North Carolina they do not appear some years until late March and early April. Should we see this data as a reflection of their reluctance to leave South Carolina and move northward due to local weather conditions, or merely the chimera of spotty evidence?

The Male Comes First

The male birds, acting as scouts, usually arrive well in advance of the females, then use the intervening time to establish themselves at the potential nesting site, to feed and to preen, all with a welcome indulgence in vocal exercise, a loud declamation of squatters' rights. This initial visit is usually of short duration. According to one ornithologist, it often lasts for not more than a single hour, often going unobserved by humans who only later may see both male and female arrive together. During this time of first arrival by the male it may sing and go in and out of a few rooms of the bird house, then finally leave, not to be seen again for several days or even a week or more. Where it goes is a point of conjecture; perhaps to the common roosting area in the vicinity of pre-season grouping. It is doubtful that the male returns to South America during this period to escort the female back to the house that he has found. Some few mention this as a possibility but have advanced no proof to substantiate such position. As in most migratory species, the male martin often preceeds the female martin, thus being no particularly unusual trait.

The busy chirp and chatter of the first Purple Martins in the early spring morning has pleasantly awakened

AN ADD-TO COM-
PLEX

DECOR

SELECTIVE STYLES

FOR THOSE PREFER-
RING HEIGHT

many a martin lover, with the message that old friends are about to return. Nothing can arouse one from bed more swiftly than this most pleasing voice of spring. Just ask any martin lover.

In instances when the females accompany the males on their first visit, bad weather may have delayed the arrival of the male scouts. It may also drive them to the box for shelter, forcing an early decision to settle down. But when both male and female martins arrive together, they will sometimes visit several houses before nesting.

The Male Selects The Site

The male usually selects the nesting territory. When visiting a bird house with multiple apartments, it will go from room to room, sometimes remaining as long as ten minutes in one, often re-entering several before making up its mind. New birds sometimes arrive and attempt to use the room that the first male had already selected. When this happens a fight ensues.

There seems to be a developed fighting instinct among members of this species, nearly always centered around the nesting site. Not only will the martin attack other birds that attempt to bother it, but the male in particular will take on any other male martin that trespasses upon its property. On the other hand, females seem to be permitted, if not encouraged, to visit, a practice which works to the advantage of unmated males. As for fighting between younger and older males, the initial act of aggression is usually by the younger male in search of new territory.

Martin battles seem to follow two strategies: an adult male sees another adult male alight on the perch in front of the room, in which case it either advances and immediately engages the intruder in fight or retreats into the room. The intruder may leave; or if he persists, the two birds may fly at one another in combat, with beak, wing and claw as weapons. Each seizes the opponent, and they fall towards the ground. Usually the two birds separate just before reaching the ground; yet occasionally the battle will continue on the ground momentarily.

If the intruder follows the owner into this room, the result is likely to be violent. Sometimes when the loser decides to leave, the other bird will not let him go. Rather, he may sit at the doorway, dangling his foe in the air below by the claw, while the latter vainly struggles to free himself. Such a fight often lasts for five or ten minutes. One instance is reported in which a male kept his opponent in this exceedingly uncomfortable position for 35 minutes, pecking him violently all the while! His hold was broken only by the disturbance of a man who happened past and frightened both into retreat.

In its most elaborate form, the fighting behavior of the martin includes three well-defined stages, referred to by some as 'calling', 'posturing', and 'attacking'. 'Calling' is done by the male and consists of a series of warning cries which range from chirping and singing to a loud rasping noise made with the beak. More aggressive still is 'posturing', which consists of a pointing motion whereby the male lowers and retracts its neck, haunches its shoulders, flattens itself somewhat and points its beak at the intruder as a clear warning gesture. At this point the bird may begin to snap its bill peevishly, as a visible and audible reinforcement of the warning posture. The third or 'attack' stage occurs when an intruder is grasped in the beak and beaten by the wings of the defender.

Fighting begins when the first males come to settle down in the colony and continues as long as new birds are arriving. It has been noted, though, that once a male Purple Martin has chosen its nesting site, it seldom attempts to trespass upon the premises of others, and its only fights are with those that seek to evict it. In any case, little permanent injury seems to result from the fighting.

In the pre-nesting period we have just described,

IN A PARKWAY

A SURE-FIRE NINE-
PLEX

27

the male martin will often be seen singing from the front of the apartment, or atop the bird house. This song can be heard especially when the male sees other birds flying over, and it seems to mean: "No trespassing here!"

Pair Formation

When the female arrives at the colony, a state of great excitement apparently arises within the male. Perched near the room selected for his mate-to-be, he lets loud, excited calls burst forth when the female alights on the porch. Once aroused, the male will follow the female excitedly from room to room, sometimes even pursuing her to another house, where he may be driven away by another male protecting its own domicile. But by noon such activity wanes and the birds begin to settle down; thus the female may spend the entire afternoon going about from room to room on a tour of inspection, while the male pays little attention to her.

When a male and female have finally accepted each other, they settle down for the season, come what may, for there seems to be little divorce among the martins. Pairing occurs with few ceremonies of formal courtship. During this period each male defends his immediate territory from the other males and develops a distinct form of vocalization which becomes an integral part of his territorial defense. These "male calls" consist of series of short chirps sung in an ascending scale and ending with a rasping note, which some have described as sounding rather like a slipping ratchet or a stick run across a picket fence. A very true description!

After pair formation has been completed, the male begins to restrict his defensive activities to one or two apartments and their porches. Frequently he is joined by the female in the task. Later, as nesting progresses, the female will tend to restrict her defense to the apartment alone. Then after egg laying has been completed, she will even permit an intruder to approach the hole, provided he

WITH ANTENNA

MAKE A SELECTION

does not try to enter.

Martins usually do not begin their nest building until several weeks after the room selection time is over, and the mates have settled down. In the intervening time male and female sit around the house, preening and sing- and generally establishing their squatter's rights. An occasional bit of excitement is provided when an intruding sparrow or some predatory bird is chased away from the house. Unfortunately the martin is not always persistent enough to prevent some enterprising sparrow from taking over an apartment in the same house as his own.

Copulation

Nest building soon begins, and during this three or four-week interval copulation takes place. Some ornithologists have observed that it is during the selection of twigs for the nest (when both sexes are on the ground) that the male will suddenly 'pounce' upon the female, striking her

A GOOD VIEW OF MALE AND FEMALE
(COURTESY JIM ELLIS, HATTIESBURG, MISS.)

suddenly on the back. She will resist initially by flying away from the male; if this occurs, he follows in lively pursuit. There insues a race around the colony in great spiralling circles until the pair returns to its house. On occasion these 'sexual flights' provide the opportunity for other males to pursue also. The original mate of the female is quick to defend his right to continue uninterruptedly by competition, and will resort to an all-out battle when another male approaches. Such fighting continues throughout the entire period of copulation.

Not all copulation takes place while the birds are on the ground. It may take place while the martins are perched on their house. As in the case of the initial formation of the pair, copulation is for the most part limited to the morning hours, observations will show.

When the female has reached the proper physiological state, she flattens herself for the male to mount, and copulation similar to that of most other birds follows. Copulation continues intermittently until the laying of the first eggs, when the female's attention must turn to incubation.

RAISING THE YOUNG

Martin eggs

The Purple Martin lays from three to eight eggs in its nest. One ornithologist checked 84 sets of martins in the vicinity of Ann Arbor, Michigan and found seven eggs in 1% of the nests, six eggs in 19%, five eggs in 54%, four eggs in 25%, and three eggs in 1%. This gives an average of just above five eggs per nest. Another study of 45 nests in Missouri yielded similar results. The writer's own experience points to a slightly lower number than that. Nevertheless, his figures may represent a local peculiarity. It may be said generally that the various studies of martin nesting habits attest to a wide margin of variation in the number of eggs which can be expected. Needless to say, such investigations of nesting habits should be left to professional ornithologists or trained, sympathetic laymen, for inexperienced investigations can, without meaning to, disturb the nest and frighten the birds from the colony for good. Any bird lover, on the other hand, can find great enjoyment in keeping a record of the number of young martins observed in each of the apartments in his colony, and this is well worth the small amount of trouble involved.

Eggs are laid singly on successive days of the week, and, once again, in the early morning. Serious martin activity definitely seems to be a morning affair, perhaps because it is cooler then.

The martin eggs are pure white, not glossy but a flat white tone. Each egg is approximately one inch long and a maximum of three-quarters of an inch wide. Its shape will vary from ovate to elliptical-ovate.

Martin egg (actual size)

Adult birds do not permit the egg shells from newly hatched young to remain in the nest. These shells are

GOURD COLONY

STYLIZED ALUM-
INUM HOUSES
(WITH TWO ENTRANCE
HOLES FOR EACH
APARTMENT)

usually eaten for their calcium content or they are carried away and dropped some distance from the box. The feces, too, are taken from the apartment daily by the adult birds. It is obvious from these two procedures alone that the Purple Martin is a very neat bird.

The Nest

The martin makes the foundation structure of its nest with dead twigs from nearby trees. These are usually gathered from the ground below the house, or from as nearby as possible.

The literature on martins cites feathers as materials used in the lining of the nest — the author has never found feathers in a martin nest, however. Examination of the nest, after summer has passed and the birds have left for South America, reveals little obvious effort to build the nest according to regular design. Some martins use much more material than others. Some fill their room with materials to a depth of several inches, while others are content merely to cover the floor, and this sparingly.

The male martin seems to be more active than the female in the gathering of nesting materials during the first few days of construction. Eventually the female lends her aid, and then she proves to do a better job than the male, who often goes about his work in a rather inept way. He will drop the materials on the way to the house or once at the house, fail to get it into the entrance hole. A frustrated male can be seen outside the doorway of his apartment with a much too wide twig in his mouth, attempting vainly to push it sideways through the doorway. This he often repeats from doorway to doorway before finally succeeding or dropping the twig in disgust. I have seen a male martin try to force a twig into as many as eight different rooms of a colony before giving up. It never occurred to him to insert it end-first! The author has gathered enough of these dropped twigs from beneath the martin house to build several nests. But he has also observed a male martin flying from apartment to apartment with a twig in its mouth, as if attempting to encourage the would-be mate to begin her building. During this period the male goes in and out of one apartment, then another, trying to tempt the female, but often to no avail.

Females seem much better oriented in their attempts at nest building. They go about their work with a degree of assurance and seldom have any trouble in getting twigs through the doorway, at least partly because they select material of a more reasonable size.

An interesting observation of nest building was made by the author when he added a new house of six apartments to his martin colony. Though both the old house, which remained on the same spot, and the new house nearby were installed on the same day, nest building occurred in the old house first. Then for some unexplainable reason, a male decided to move the nest to the new house. He made numerous trips moving twig upon twig to the new apartment from the old. Occasionally his work

AMONG THE PINES

AMONG THE MIMOSAS

was interrupted by the need to defend the former nest from a second male before the nest was entirely removed. It was a curious situation. Indeed, the writer could not determine whether the frenzied male really was swapping apartments or was simply an interloper stealing twigs from a nearby neighbor. Banding alone could tell.

As nest building proceeds, the male martin soon loses interest in the whole affair; the work is left entirely to the female from that time on, although he will speak a few notes of encouragement from the housetop as the chore continues.

Since the martin nest is rather coarsely constructed, it has nothing of the beauty which some birds can impart to their nest. It is merely functional, and serves its intended purpose with adequacy. The framework of twigs, usually lined with leaves, is gathered from trees within the nearby vicinity. Sometimes roots, grass, or pine straw is used. A close examination by the author of twelve nests revealed the following materials: oak leaves, elm

**GOURD COLONY
(THE AUTHOR TAPES
CONVERSATION)**

JUGS AND GOURDS

leaves, pine straw, mahonia leaves, and grass. All of these were found within a fifty-foot radius of the bird colony. Pieces of shell and glass were found mixed within the remains of uneaten insect wings in the center of the nest. Shell, it will be recalled, is eaten by the birds to supply a need for calcium in their diet.

The following photographs show martin nests which were removed from a martin house after the season was over. Observe the variation in thickness. A mound of dirt can be seen across the front of the nest, presumably to prevent the eggs from rolling out. The deepest cavity of the nest is towards the back, affording additional protection to the eggs and the female during incubation.

Various observers have recorded the length of egg incubation, and found it varies from 12 to 20 days. The average is 13 to 14 days.

The female performs the incubation alone, but the feeding of the young is undertaken jointly by both sexes. While incubation continues, the male is an attentive mate,

45

twittering about the box, flying past the hole, and singing low, emphatic, and prolonged notes as if in direct communication with the female.

The female incubates about 70% of the day, and during her brief absences the male guards the nest. During incubation, the martins' singing is reduced and much less flight about the colony can be observed. More attentive care of the nest is now necessary.

Though the male is seen entering and leaving the room, even remaining for several minutes while the mate is away, there is no proof that males ever incubate the eggs, even though males have been known to enter the room for short periods of time even before the nesting period begins. One observer recorded a male spending only four minutes of a two-hour period in the box; another spent seven, 14 and 16 minutes in the room. On every occasion, the male entered as soon as the female departed and stayed inside only until the female came back again.

A later record by the same observer revealed a

cooperative venture in which three males stood guard while the female was away. The first entered the room as soon as the female left, stayed a minute or two, and came back out. A long delay followed, and it left the house. Immediately a second male took over the guard duty, now sitting just inside the apartment with his head in the doorway. He was then replaced by a third male who stayed even longer just inside the apartment.

Incubation usually begins after the last egg is laid. On cool days the adults spend the night in the apartment with the eggs. This raises the temperature to some extent. Conversely, on warm days they remain outside much longer — probably for their own comfort.

Incubation sessions usually vary from four to 15 minutes, but sometimes they may last as long as 20 minutes. This on-and-off incubation keeps the egg temperature rather constant. Records of the number of incubation sessions per day varies considerably. In one study the number of incubations amounted to: 24, 20, 15,

17, 25, and 30 sessions per day (with an average of 21.8 times). The average length of time was 12 minutes per session.

Renesting

Though the Purple Martin usually lays only one set of eggs each year, it has been known to lay another set if the first ones are destroyed. One instance of the destruction of eggs occurred during the early part of the nesting season, and the nesting process was repeated by the same pair of birds. But another study reports the same occurrence late in the season and cites no attempt to lay new eggs once the first brood had been destroyed by a predator. A third observer recorded 80 instances in which newly-hatched young succumbed in mid-June and in which the parents did re-nest. From these observations it would seem that after a considerable period of the nesting season has elapsed, re-nesting will not be attempted. Prevailing

VERTED DISHPAN

MARTIN LOVER'S
DREAM

49

local conditions must also play a part in the adult martin's decision to re-nest or not.

Opinions differ about the number of broods raised by martins in a single year. Some observers have reported double broods, others claim that one is the maximum for a season. Unfortunately not all the evidence is equally reliable and so the matter remains uncertain. This writer feels compelled to note that he has never discovered any conclusive evidence for the raising of more than a single brood during a season, and his viewpoint represents the consensus of ornithologists who have expressed themselves on this matter.

One reference cites as many as three broods (in Louisiana) for a season, but this observation was made a hundred years ago by Audubon and no scientific evidence for his belief is cited.

A leading ornithologist reports on the basis of studies conducted by means of banding, that he never encountered more than one brood per year, although

BEAUTY

RESTRICTIVE EN-
VIRONS

51

sometimes a stray bird has been known to lay an additional egg or two late in the summer season. He argues strongly for one brood: "I can definitely say that there is absolutely no evidence of the species raising a second brood. Sometimes I have had new pairs come to the house late in the season and raise after other pairs were through with theirs. Had the birds not been banded, one might well have supposed that these late nesters constituted a second brood." This statement probably explains all the reported, but mistaken, instances of a second brood.

After hatching, the young martins will remain in the nest for three or four weeks or even longer. After they have become strong enough to fly, they will return to the nest only for a few additional days. The writer has observed parents and young returning to the vicinity of the box each day for a short while, even after the young have gained their independence. They would alight momentarily, then depart to a nearby television antenna for play and conversation. But from all indications the family instinct is not well developed among the martins, and almost immediately the family breaks up for good.

Feeding The Young

Newly hatched martins are not especially attractive for the first few days of their life. They are entirely devoid of down, and they are hardly strong enough to rouse themselves from the bottom of the nest, where they are curled. They respond only to the external stimulus of sound or touch, and weakly lift their heads to utter a cheep or receive food from their parents.

The feeding of the young is perhaps one of the most interesting habits of the martins that one can observe. If the birds arrive in the middle of February, by the late June and early July period little heads will begin to appear in the doorways. Sometimes one, sometimes two, even three or four at once! And as they grow older, each fights more vigorously to get its head through the

A SWINGING DELIGHT

WORSHIPFUL
ATMOSPHERE

MOTHER FEEDING THE YOUNG

(COURTESY S. A. GRIMES, JACKSONVILLE, FLA.)

door for the food which its busy parents provide. The adult birds must now work rapidly, and repeated trips are required to keep these little mouths satisfied. During this period, the parents can pay little attention to one another, since they are totally absorbed with their brood. Singing and fighting all but cease. When the young are about 12 days old, the adults give up sleeping in the box and roost in trees instead.

One authority logged the feeding trips made to a single martin apartment during a certain day and observed a parent bird arriving every 30 seconds with food. Another watched a colony of eight pairs of birds from four a.m. to eight p.m.; during this time the parents visited their offspring 3,277 times, or an average of 205 times for each pair! The males made 1,454 visits and the females made 1,823 visits.

Others have reported feedings every 20 seconds. From such data one can conclude easily that many thousands of insects are consumed daily by these helpful little birds. It is safe to conclude that the diet of one adult martin may include many mosquitos a day. When one adds to that the insects caught for feeding of the young, the value of this bird as an insect eradicator is great.

Growth Of The Young

Feathers are grown by the young martins from the 12th to the 20th day. The first appearance of fear reactions do not occur until the 14th or 15th day, when the young huddle silently in the back of the nest, quiet and ready to peck at any strange object that enters their field of vision. As they grow older, they lose all tendency to be silent — in fact quite the opposite! It has been found, too, that on the 15th or 16th day the young birds will return to the apartment if placed on the front porch of the box.

The young stay in the nest roughly 20 to 30 days. The time varies somewhat with the colony. Normally they leave at the age of about 28 days. By now, their feathers have developed sufficiently for the young martins to fly. Sometimes the parents have difficulty in making the young bird venture forth on its own. But if it can only be lured onto the porch, the parents find a way to crowd it off into the air. Then it has no choice but to fly. Away it goes.

Brooding

The female broods the young for about the same length of time that she spends in incubating the eggs, 12 to 20 days. During this period she seldom visits the nest without brooding the young. The male often helps to feed the young and sometimes remains on the nest for a short period of time. After the young are about five days old the brooding time is reduced from around 70% to 50% and about the tenth day stops all together. If the air temperature drops, however, the adults will brood the young for a longer duration.

Sometimes the young birds become overly ambitious and fall from the house before they are ready to fly. This may happen when they are pushed out by the other young, or in the process of fighting for food. An over-infestation of mites has been known to drive the young from the nest. So has the intense heat of the sun. In such circumstances the parent birds will light on the ground near their fallen offspring for a while, but soon they must abandon them to become the food of prowling cats or other predatory animals.

One long-time Purple Martin enthusiast has replaced hundreds of fallen young birds into their houses (which he makes from hollow gourds) by means of a long cane with a notched groove at the end. In this groove he places the leg of the young bird and raises the martin to the hole of an apartment, where he gently rakes it off into the nest. The writer has observed his replacing two young birds by this method (see photograph, next page). The enthusiast was asked how he know which apartment the

baby bird had come from. To this he replied, "I do not know. I merely place them back into any apartment and never have I found a parent bird who refused to feed them." Furthermore, he never found a dead bird in a nest at the end of the season. One sometimes hears that adult birds refuse to care for their young after they have been handled by human hands. This notion is quite untrue; it has also been refuted by bird banders, who find that the handling of birds has no effect on their care by parent birds.

When Male and Female Look Alike

When all of the newly hatched birds, males and females, grow enough to migrate with the flock at the end of the summer, they appear to be females in their coloration.

According to A. C. Bent, the males do not acquire their deep purple feathers until their first post-nuptial molt, at about 18 months of age. This means the second summer before we see the male in full dark coloration.

This causes great difficulty in keeping count of male and female birds from year to year. So, don't be fooled about the sex of your martins. Even well known ornithologists have banded seeming females only to have them return the next summer as full fledged males in purple splendor.

THE DIET OF THE PURPLE MARTIN

Since the martins eat almost nothing but insects, their value to a neighborhood is significant. One source relates the story of a peach grower in Georgia who deliberately set up rows of martin houses in his peach orchard and thereby protected his crop from the curculio beetle that had caused millions of dollars' damage elsewhere.

An ornithologist cites evidence of a single martin which ate 400 flies in a single day. Elsewhere the martin has been said to eat 2000 mosquitos in a day.

One authoritative study states that "Since martins are very active, requiring a large amount of food, the number of insects they destroy in order to get sufficient nourishment is not only beyond calculation but almost beyond comprehension."

Insects that are commonly consumed by the Purple Martin include: house flies, mosquitos, ants, wasps, beetles (especially weevils), and dragonflies. One of the insects most often observed in feeding of the martin young is the dragonfly – but perhaps that is only because the dragonfly is large enough to be easily detected. It is an interesting sight to watch a martin's tiny mouth trying to gulp down a large dragonfly; often the dragonfly wings are left dangling outside the young bird's mouth. One begins to wonder whether the young martin will fly away with dragonfly wings! An observer related to the writer that he had seen a parent martin bring two dragonflies to a nest at the same time, feeding one to a baby martin in one room and one to another in an adjoining room. In this case the feeding of young in another apartment probably resulted from the young bird's moving to another apartment. Not infrequently this happens when the apartment becomes overcrowded and a vacant one is nearby and available.

An exhaustive study of the diet of Purple Martins revealed that spiders were seldom found. The percentage of hymenoptera in the diet was 23% – mostly wasps and ants, with only a few bees. These findings refute the story that martins destroy honey bees, for only five bees were found in 200 stomachs examined, and every one of these was a drone. Flies amounted to 16%, both houseflies and long-legged crane flies. Bugs amounted to 15%, including stink-bugs, tree hoppers, and black bugs. Beetles amounted to 12%, including May, ground, dung, cotton-boll, and clover weevil beetles. Some moths and butterflies were found, and dragonflies were found in 65 stomachs, with some having nothing but dragonflies in them.

A study of seasonal variation of the insect diet of the Purple Martin revealed an interesting pattern. The study was made through comparison of the stomach contents of Purple Martins taken in a sample of an area 20 miles square, largely during the morning hours. This data was compared to a sampling of available insects in the area collected in the same territory by means of a ten-inch insect net held out the window of a rapidly moving automobile. These data were compared for early, middle, and late breeding seasons of the martin. The conclusions show that beetles are a common food for the martin throughout all the seasons, while flies disappeared from the diet after June; the greatest variety of food was taken by the martin late in the season, in August.

The study also showed that insects available to the Purple Martin as food were much more abundant in August than earlier — three times better than in June. The authors admit that the sampling technique was crude, for dragonflies could avoid the nets, while they could not avoid the birds; windy weather was avoided in catching insect samples, while the martin has to catch insects in heavy winds as well; and the net samples were taken only at low altitudes, while martins catch many of their insects well up in the air.

The evidence provided by this study can be taken to give a general picture of the martin's feeding habits. Three observations prove interesting: first, the food supply approaches maximum at a period when energy demands of

A NEW LOOK AT THE COUNTY SEAT

(COURTESY O. D. CRAWFORD, CANTON, MISS.)

the birds become maximal. Second, in August adult Purple Martins begin their annual moult, and after this they must shift to the premigration physiology, which demands the building up of layers of fat. Both the growth of new feathering and the accumulation of fat require above-normal energy at this period. And third, adults and first-year birds begin to move south. Thus, these birds leave at a time of a maximum abundance of food and move south to an area of a similar abundance of food.

To some extent, the martin counteracts its own beneficial value to man. Particularly is this true when one considers that martins eat dragonflies, and that dragonflies themselves eat mosquitos. Furthermore the martin usually catches its food well up in the air, while many mosquitos seldom reach such heights. Yet another martin observer points out that parent birds are not particularly interested in catching dragonflies until the young are half grown and suggests that they may be fed to provide roughage in the diet. Furthermore, adult dragonflies may be useful in that

MOTHER AND YOUNG AT FEEDING TIME
(COURTESY S.A. GRIMES, JACKSONVILLE, FLA.)

they eat harmful insects like mosquitos, yet the young dragonflies destroy fish, thus tending to neutralize the dragonfly's overall value to man.

In any case, rather than erect martin houses specifically for the purpose of mosquito eradication, martin lovers build them simply to attract these wonderful birds for amusement and entertainment; for, as one perceptive ornithologist rightly stated, they are "just a fine bird to have around."

NOT TO BE CONFUSED WITH THE "BEE" MARTIN

To many laymen, particularly in the rural districts, the Eastern Kingbird, well known member of the flycatcher family, is often confused with the Purple Martin. In fact it is commonly, though incorrectly, called the "bee martin." Through careful observation, however, it is possible to distinguish the two. The "bee martin" frequents an environment much closer to the ground than does the Purple Martin. It particularly delights in the fence row, while the Purple Martin is seldom ever seen in these environs. While its size may approach that of the Purple Martin, its color and living habits make it easily distinguishable from the Purple Martin.

The "bee martin" (Kingbird) earned its name, not surprisingly, from a reputed fondness for the denizens of the bee hive. But studies have shown that the Eastern Kingbird, like the Purple Martin, usually eats the drone bees, perhaps because they are easier to catch than the others. Thus, neither part of its "nickname" is truly justified.

One contributing factor to this mistaken identity is the trait of each species to attack large birds of prey that fly too close to their domain. Particularly is this true of the attack upon the hawk and this is known to happen at distances of a half-mile or more away. This is such a distinctive trait of both the "bee" martin and the Purple Martin that farmers will hasten to verify this fact and even claim that they raise Purple Martins to protect their chickens from this bird of prey, the hawk. The author himself has watched many attacks of this type take place and has seen both "bee" martins and Purple Martins in the same attack. Their swift girations are not easily countered by these larger birds who retreat as quickly as possible.

ENEMIES OF THE PURPLE MARTIN

There are a few pesky birds that have become enemies of the martins by trying to take over their nesting places, especially apartments in man-made bird houses. The principal natural rivals are the English Sparrow* and the Starling.†

Both interlopers cause considerable trouble to the martins, who must struggle with them for nesting rights, and to the martin lovers, who are faced with the continual problem of ridding the yard of these pests. One great deterrent to the nesting of the two birds is removal of the martin house during the winter, to be replaced only when

---

*The English Sparrow or House Sparrow is a member of the Old-World Weaver Finch Family. It was brought to America from England in 1850, became established, spread rapidly, and is now a serious pest. Do not confuse this bird with our native sparrows, which currently are placed in one or more different families or subfamilies, depending upon the authority one wishes to follow.

†The European Starling was introduced into New York in 1890 and now has become common throughout the country. Not considered as much a nuisance as the English Sparrow, it is still undesirable as a yard bird.

the martins return in the spring. This prevents the nesting of any rival birds before the martins arrive. However, sparrows may commence building almost the very hour that the martin house is erected. The battle with the English Sparrow is eternal. A sparrow trap would be little help in such a situation, for there will always be too many sparrows in the neighborhood to deal with. Some authorities claim that a single pair of sparrows is the maximum number that will build in a martin colony, for the presence of this pair will deter other sparrows from building there, too. If that is true, then one can perhaps afford to sacrifice a single martin apartment to the pesky little bird without undue worry. The starling is a bit more wary. Consequently it is more easily discouraged by human beings than the House Sparrow (but unfortunately not by the Purple Martin).

Eastern Bluebirds, Tree Swallows, and House Wrens are sometimes mentioned as competitors of the martins for living space. On rare occasions, for example, the wren has been known to enter the Purple Martin house and throw out the eggs, despite the martins' efforts to frighten it away. But even though such unusual cases do occur, it would be unfair to put the wren, tree swallow, and bluebird in the same category as the House Sparrow or the European Starling. One would be delighted to share the martin house with such fine birds as these (even though the Purple Martin isn't).

The writer had one apartment taken over by a pair of crested flycatchers. One day when walking by the house he noted a snake skin, recently shed (for it was very pliable), beneath the house on the ground. His immediate thought was that the snake had gotten into the house. Upon reading about flycatchers, however, to his surprise the statement was made that crested flycatchers had a peculiar trait of finding snake skins to place across the front of their home to frighten the other birds away. He knew, then, that this is what had been done and the skin had been blown down from the house by the wind.

Another enemy of the martin is the screech owl, which causes its damage in stealth under the protection of darkness. The screech owl has been known to devour as many as half a dozen young martins in an evening before appeasing its appetite. The owl's method of kill is to thrust one leg as far into the apartment as possible and seize a defenseless martin in its talons. The writer sadly attributes to such a cause the sudden disappearance one night of several of his young martins. A word of warning then: if a loud frightened twitter of martins is heard during the night, make haste to the bird house with a flashlight and frighten this harmful predator away. The resounding cries of martins under attack is easy enough to distinguish from the contented notes of their usual midnight chatter.

A quite exceptional case was reported by another observer however: Screech owls were seen nesting in one compartment in a large martin house, while ten Purple Martins occupied the remaining rooms. After the owl family departed a pair of martins promptly moved in.

From this it might appear that not all screech owls devour young martins. But more likely the incident took place before the nesting season of the Purple Martins when there were no young birds to devour.

By far the greatest deterrent of the Purple Martin is the weather, for martins cannot withstand any great amount of cold. A sudden cold spell has been known to eradicate an entire colony, and when this happens, it is usually a long while before the martins return again to that locality.

In some years there seem to be fewer male birds than others. This was clearly true in 1965, probably attributed to a sudden storm during migration or to a cold spell that caught the vanguard as it arrived in this country. Several years are required to overcome such an occurrence, and reoccurrences of such severe weather conditions can prolong recovery in numbers for years. Persistent cold rains one year all but eliminated the Purple Martin from northern New Jersey to southern New Hampshire. This territory was not reestablished for many years, according to reports. A severe cold spell, of course, means a paucity of the insect life necessary to support the martin colony. The martin's digestion is very rapid and consequently it requires a large diet of insects at all times. Two or three days of severe cold can reduce its food supply as to be fatal, particularly if stored fat has been consumed.

One observer reports that long rains resulted in the death of 30 young birds and two adult birds in a New England martin colony; the remaining martins deserted the house, leaving 12 unhatched eggs. Similarly, in one year a cold rainy spell virtually eliminated martins in eastern Massachusetts and contiguous parts of New England, none of which were substantially reinhabited for many years. Often when martins do return after such a disaster they find the house full of English sparrows, are disquieted, and move on to other nesting places.

Periods of inclement weather can occur late in the year and then of course they produce the highest mortality. A martin fancier who had been observing martins for 15 years, reported that a three-day period of cold, cloudy, and rainy weather set in around May 9 of one year; and when the period of inclemency was over and warmer weather returned, 33 of 40 adult birds were dead, an 80% mortality rate. Another set-back came in 1960, when a similar five-day period killed 40% of the martins. In both cases the birds starved to death. The most disconcerting aspect of these experiences is the martin enthusiast's inability to change the weather. Nor can he hope to provide food for the martin as in the case of other neighborhood birds, for the Purple Martin diet consists almost exclusively of insects. Some martin fanciers report isolated instances of martins alighting in the yard to eat suet and egg shells with other birds, and in an emergency such feedings may be worth a try. Suet, of course, can be obtained free or for a few cents at a neighborhood meat market. It is well to note that care should be taken not to prolong such feeding after the cold weather has subsided.

It could easily cause the martins to develop a dependence upon an unnatural, artificial diet which would leave them in a condition too weak for insect retrieval. At the close of the summer they would have built up insufficient reserve to make the long journey to South America and probably die of exhaustion during the long flight back. A sign conspicuously posted in the Everglades National Park in Florida applies to this situation as well: IT IS MISTAKEN KINDNESS TO FEED ANY WILDLIFE HERE, AND IT IS PROHIBITED TO DO SO, BECAUSE THERE IS AMPLE NATURAL FOOD. ARTIFICIAL FEEDING ENCOURAGES VULNERABILITY TO DISEASE, DEPENDENCE UPON MAN, AND AN UNNATURAL SITUATION.

Equally dangerous to the martins is the intense summer heat, which often kills the young outright. We stress here the value of using a white paint on martin houses to reflect the summer heat; also of providing adequate ventilation holes in the apartments of the bird house.

Frequently the parent birds collect green leaves and place them in the nest; presumably this raises the humidity within the nest and thereby decreases evaporation. Both male and female birds can be seen fetching leaves, but the chore largely falls to the male and will constitute a major portion of his morning activity in the hottest part of the summer season. The author, using his field glasses, watched a male fly from the apartment to an adjoining elm tree and wrestle for five minutes with a green leaf, trying to break it from the solid hold that it seemed to have. Finally, in disgust, the bird flew away to another tree where it had more success. The leaves are never brought in during the evenings, even in the hottest weather. The writer has found leaves many times when he cleared out the nests from the martin boxes at the close of the season. In some instances a few of the leaves were found to be still slightly green, indicating that the martins had continued to fetch them almost until the time of departure.

Three more enemies of the Purple Martin must be mentioned here. First is the squirrel. He is perhaps more a problem in town than elsewhere, since there, martin boxes are more likely to be located near trees or buildings. The squirrel's usual means of approach is to leap to the martin house from a nearby height (a tree or building), kill the young birds, destroy the eggs, and even take over one or more of the apartments to raise its young. The martin enthusiast should bear this in mind when selecting the site for his martin box.

A second class of enemies of the Purple Martin is the snake, particularly the non-poisonous rat snakes and black snakes. These have been known to climb the poles and devour both young and eggs. This is less likely to happen in the city where there are few known snakes. One rural martin lover was awakened by the frightened chatter coming from her martin house early in the morning. Running to inspect, she found a large black rat ("chicken") snake, already leaving with a young martin in its mouth.

(It was of course too late to attempt a rescue, but it was also too late for the snake . . .)

House cats form a third category of enemies of the Purple Martin. It is extremely important to protect the martin house from cats. Like squirrels, they jump to the bird house from any nearby height, although not as well as do the squirrels. The writer recalls a martin enthusiast who was aroused early one morning by unusual chattering from the birds, and found a stray cat perched upon the roof of the martin house, twenty feet above the ground. A garden hose happened to be connected and lying beneath the bird house. Cats, of course dislike water even more than they like young birds. There was no place for the feline to run. The severe sprinkling he could not stand, and his only alternative was a long leap to the ground. Such situations are better prevented than remedied. As a precaution against all kinds of climbing animals, one can attach a circular "cat-stopper" half way up the pole which supports the bird house, or attach a metal sheet around the pole to cover a three-foot area. If it is painted to match the pole, it will not appear distasteful from below. A word of precaution here. The metal sheet bent around the pole may not prevent the snake from climbing over it, nor is it true that a metal pole will always prevent his climb. The snake can climb metal or wooden poles. So, the best preventive is a circular (or square) sheet of metal at right angles to the pole, similar to those placed on anchor lines or cables that prevent rats from climbing across from the dock to the ocean liners.

LONGEVITY

One frequently wonders just how long a martin lives. Is it a short-lived bird or does it live longer than many of the other species? Longevity is difficult to determine and only through bird banding studies can one determine with any degree of accuracy the life expectancy.

Several studies have been made in this respect, but we hasten to add that no one knows the longest life span of the Purple Martin, but only the longest *known* span of life. However, these studies do give a fair average life expectancy and prove to be most interesting data in helping to complete our story of the Purple Martin.

Allen and Nice report studies of 46 martins banded as nestlings and recovered from one to six years later with the greatest age attained in their studies being eight years.

A more recent study, 1966, of Franks who analyzed the banding records of 487 martins as reported from the Fish and Wildlife Service of Laurel, Maryland, shows thirteen recaptured at a known age of at least five years with ten of the 13 between five and seven years, two at seven years and nine months, and one, banded on July 1, 1933 was found dead in the spring of 1947, being of known age of 13 years and nine months.

This we believe to be a record in longevity for the Purple Martin and is a record substantiated by the "Report to Hunter Card" of the Fish and Wildlife Service, an astounding revelation.

From these data we can conclude that the span of life of the Purple Martin is between 0 and 13 years, nine months, at least, and even beyond perhaps.

MIGRATION

Why Migration?

After its summer visit of from three to six months (depending upon the latitude) the Purple Martin can be expected to leave even more suddenly than it arrived — off to South America (and to the Amazon Basin in particular) for a sojourn in a warmer climate.

Scholars as well as laymen have often conjectured about the reasons for the martin's migration. What are the advantages? What patterns do martins follow as they migrate?

Many theories have been proposed to answer these questions. One of these is the "Northern Home Theory." According to it, the North American continent was the original home of certain birds and that during the Pleistocene Era or earlier, they were forced to seek milder climates and occasionally migrated southward. Only later did they return to their homeland of North America for breeding. Thus the martins return north in the summer.

No scientific account (there have been many) for the migration of birds is yet convincing. Migration is conceivably related to the birds' habitat in an earlier era. Unfortunately, enough is not yet known about the phenomenon of 'instinct' to describe the nature of such a relationship. Ornithologists have noted that the migratory species often winter in a geographic area that is ecologically related to their breeding grounds. This would mean the selection of comparable wintering sites in South America.

The immediate reasons and advantages of present-day migrations are more obvious. One is related to climate As we have already mentioned, the Purple Martin often cannot withstand even a short cold spell; it must seek a climate that will permit survival through the winter season, where sufficient insect life is available. Sometimes this necessitates many hundreds, or even thousands of miles of travel. These geographical exchanges make possible a great variety of bird diets and permit a build-up of certain vitamins, minerals, and so on, necessary to the raising of the young.

Timing Of The Migration

How do martins decide when to migrate? Weather is certainly an important factor. Food shortages, too, may cause an early migration. Some think the variation in arrival times is almost exclusively due to this factor. The time of year for departure to new quarters is also directly related to the breeding cycle of the Purple Martin. The exact day on which the migratory flight begins may be decided by wind direction or a change in temperature.

The Martin's Sense Of Direction

The Purple Martin's sense of direction, like that of

the homing pigeon, is something of a marvel. The fact that it can journey to South America every winter and yet return to the same bird house in the United States is nothing short of miraculous.

Many tests have been made of this homing instinct. In northern Michigan on one occasion, a female adult martin was removed from its nest containing young birds and was transported to Ann Arbor, 235 miles to the north, where it was released at 10:40 p.m. The next morning it was back on the nest again at 7:15 a.m. During the night the sky had been completely overcast by a double layer of clouds, making it quite unlikely that the bird had been able to use celestial navigation to find its way. Even though the observation of celestial bodies may at times play some part in bird navigation, yet an intimate timing mechanism peculiar to birds seems also to play a part, as does the ability to recognize certain features of the earth's surface and to remember migration routes from year to year.

Other explanations of the martin's sense of direction have been offered. According to one, a specially developed form of perception allows the birds to store up memory impressions of every twist and turn of the journey and reverse themselves on their return flight, being directed in their original flight by others of the species. A second hypothesis, perhaps rather fanciful, is that the birds can sense the earth's magnetic field and thereby acquire a compasslike sense of direction. The flight pattern of the Purple Martin, along with that of other migratory species, has also been related to the clockwise deflections of winds from the equator in the northern hemisphere (Coriolis effect).

The very fact that many birds migrate by night does tend to refute the theory that the birds observe and remember the terrain over which they pass. Starlight and moonlight may permit some observations, of course. Slightly more puzzling are what orientation points could be used in crossing the ocean. Here, wind and wave direction, islands, reefs, atolls, cloud movement, temperature and humidity, fog banks, and so on, have been suggested.

Flight Pattern

Birds often have a flight pattern that is peculiar to their species alone. Some are regular in their flight pattern, always going in a straight line; others will follow an up-and-down trajectory, combined with a "flap and coast" pattern. The Purple Martin, though, has a pattern that is unique. While it can go in a straight line of flight and does when proceeding across country or across water, yet its local pattern of insect catching is quite different. Under these more normal circumstances, the martin's flight resembles that of the tree swallow, for it sails in rather small circles 20 to 100 feet in diameter and alternates between rapid flapping and gliding. The tail is used almost continuously to maneuver.

The wing flapping of the Purple Martin has been clocked at 4.4 times per second. This gives it one of the faster rates of wing motion known. The average speed of its flight has been calculated at 20 miles per hour, though this speed can be increased if need be. One ornithologist, in fact, removed 16 Purple Martins from their nesting sites, to distances of 175 to 234 miles, and found that their average speed on the return was 27 miles per hour.

Body Fuel Stored For Migratory Flights

Shortly before birds begin a major migration they amass considerable quantities of fat, either just beneath the skin, or in concentrated fat deposits within the abdominal cavity.

Fats supply nearly twice as much energy per unit of weight as carbohydrates or proteins, and it is thus an obvious economy for a flying animal to rely on fats as stored foods. The stored fat of birds is transferred quickly into the blood stream for oxidation in muscles or elsewhere, as needed. On a long flight appreciable quantities of the stored fat are thus consumed.

A species may build up as much as 17% of the body weight in fat. On a trip across the Gulf of Mexico from South America the fat may be reduced as much as 7%. Those flying longer distances have been known to build up fat content to as much as 30%. This build-up of fat not only permits the Purple Martin to endure the long flight between continents, but gives him enough reserve to sustain himself for a period after arrival at his destination, in the event that the insect availability is initially inadequate.

Fall Migration

It is not as easy to log the fall migration of the Purple Martin, for the date of hatching will vary even within a single community, reflecting a variation in nesting dates. The author has observed the last birds leaving from his martin house around the end of July, while his friends continued to notice martins for two or three weeks, in the same part of southern United States. Generally speaking, one may expect the departure to begin as soon as possible after the last young birds have learned to fly. This seems to hold true over much of the migration range of the Purple Martin.

The problem of establishing the date of the martin's departure at a given location is made all the more difficult by the visits of transient martins, already in migration, that may stop over briefly in route.

Again we turn to a well known ornithologist, Professor George Lowery, for his observations on migration. On the basis of his experience in banding hundreds of Purple Martins, he finds that the bird never returns to the martin box during the rest of that season after leaving it, not even momentarily.

The author has to admit that he has been led to

believe otherwise from his own observations. Martins are frequently seen to alight on the bird houses after all of the young are out of the nest. In some cases they seem to be exactly the birds which had long occupied the house. Quite recently, the writer observed a colony of martins living in his own back yard, four adults and seven young birds which they raised during the season. After the young learned to fly, all the martins ceased living in the box, yet every afternoon late for about two weeks thereafter he observed exactly eleven martins that would light upon a nearby television antenna, occasionally flying to the bird house where they would stop briefly. Thus, without the proof of banded birds, it seems difficult to accept the view that martins never return once they have left the box.

Fall Gatherings

The fall migration back to South America extends throughout a rather long period. In preparation for the

GATHERING FOR
FALL DEPARTURE

Photo courtesy Humble Oil & Refining Company.

AN EVENING SCENE
JUST BEFORE DE-
PARTURE FOR
SOUTH AMERICA

Photo courtesy Humble Oil & Refining Company.

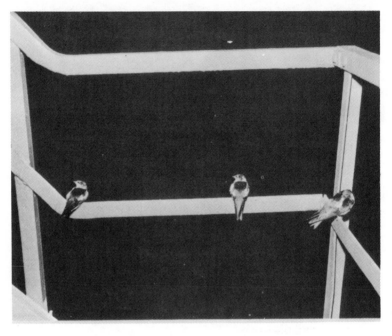

CAUGHT BY SURPRISE! (COURTESY HUMBLE OIL CO -

BATON ROUGE, LA.)

A CLOSE-UP OF
FALL GATHERING IN EVENING

(COURTESY HUMBLE
OIL CO. BATON
ROUGE, LA)

Photo courtesy Humble   Oil & Refining Company

CLOSE-UP OF NIGHT
ROOST, ALL IMMA-
TURE MALES AND
FEMALES

LOOKING UP ON A
NIGHT GATHERING
FOR FALL DEPART
URE

Photo courtesy Humble Oil & Refining Company.

BATON ROUGE, LA.

trip, there is the build-up of a huge flock, as pairs and pairs and pairs of the martins join for the flight south. There are many reports from across the country as to the vastness of these flocks of Purple Martins readying themselves for departure. Ornithological studies of such gatherings have been made, among other places, in Chicago; Tucson; Washington, D.C.; Baton Rouge; North Carolina; South Carolina; Florida; Cape May, New Jersey; St. Louis; and eastern Kansas. We have selected four of these for discussion because of their size and because of the care exercised in the observation.

One writer in Florida has observed a flock of Purple Martins that covered as wide a territory as nine miles. It must have contained more than a hundred thousand martins and was seen passing over Dade County one early November day.

Another observer mentions the congregation of martins in Baton Rouge, Louisiana, in early August in an estimated flock of 14,000 birds, this time on the tanks of an oil refining company. The first such gatherings were on cylindrical tanks. Later, when the tanks were removed, the birds moved to another part of the refinery, as the following photographs show.

A third report of this kind is also worth citing here. This took place during World War II, when Purple Martins gathered at Washington, D.C., by the thousands in a gradual build-up before the fall migration departure. They began arriving in late July and early August and would come in every evening from twelve to 33 minutes before sunset, gathering close together on electrical wires. It is interesting to note that the first birds that appeared were largely male adults. The birds that came later were almost entirely females and younger birds. At times they would all suddenly leave the wires as though by a common impulse, circle around in the air, and return to the wires, finally to depart as a group into some adjoining trees for the evening roost. The birds would awaken early each morning and would depart from the trees by 5:15 a.m. An ornithologist studying this flock reported the following schedule as typical: before 4 a.m., entirely silent; 4:03 a.m., first notes heard; 4:35 a.m., a chorus begins; 4:40 a.m., restlessness begins and movement from branch to branch; 4:55 a.m., first bird takes to the wing; 5:00 a.m., about 1000 birds leave; 5:02 a.m., 3000 to 4000 birds leave; others continually depart; 5:15 a.m., all are gone.

This activity continued until early August, by which time the number had reached an estimated 35,000. Suddenly they began to leave for South America. By August 20, only 12,000 remained in the flock, and the number dropped rapidly until by August 24 only 150 were left, and all these disappeared the following day.

Finally we might mention a martin roost observed during late August in the western part of the country. Forming in cottonwood groves, it eventually grew in size to an estimated 10,000. As in the other case already described, the martins would arrive in groups and depart in groups, rather than leaving en masse. Earlier in the summer the martins came in without the encroachment of other birds into their flock. By September 18, however, they were accompanied by a Vaux Swift (Chaetura Vauxi) and later a few other swifts. Here, as in the other cases, as the group became larger they took longer to go to the roost. The observer described the flight pattern of this flock as chiefly a counter-clockwise movement, although sometimes it would change to clockwise, leaving a long curving 'wake' of stragglers, which gave the picture of a whip being waved slowly in the sky. With each descent of the formation, large numbers of martins settled in the cottonwoods. Such flights were repeated until all the birds were at roost. He noted too that group division within the mass of martins was evident throughout the fall.

The author of this western report kept close observation of the roost when migration began after September 13, making daily visits to estimate the number of martins which remained. His findings were as follows:

September 22:	13,000 martins counted at the roost
September 23:	1,000 martins counted at the roose (stormy weather, martins dispersed)
September 24:	5,000 martins at the roost (migration has substantially begun)
September 27:	4,000 martins at the roost
September 28:	2,000 martins at the roost
September 29:	1,000 martins at the roost
September 30:	500 martins at the roost
October 1:	250 martins at the roost
October 2:	62 (counted) martins at the roost
October 3:	Only two remaining martins were seen

From this we see that within about ten days time the entire roost had completely departed from the area.

One may raise the question, whether any Purple Martins lag behind in this country during the winter, especially in the lower part of Florida and in the Keys. (Why would this not be a temptation?) Surprisingly enough, there seem to be no related reports of such a phenomenon. Observers claim to have seen small numbers of Purple Martins in Orlando, Florida as late as December 18 and have considered these possibly to be birds wintering in North America. But the martins seen in Florida surely were only belated migrants. Studies of bird migration from Florida indicate that all Purple Martins eventually leave that state entirely.

On the following map we have listed the latest dates for the departure of Purple Martins from each state, where this information could be obtained. For a few areas no information was available. We invite the reader to chart the martin departure dates in his own vicinity and compare these with the data shown on the following page.

Purple Martins Do Cross The Gulf Of Mexico

One of the most fascinating questions to arise in a study of the Purple Martin was whether it crossed the Gulf of Mexico in its flight between the Americas, or whether,

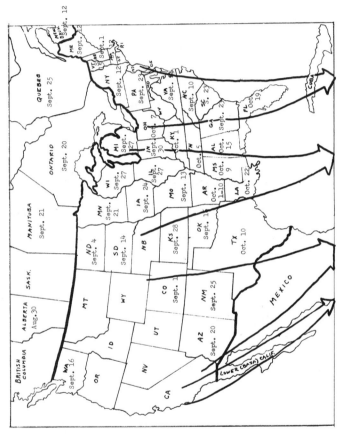

Some of the latest departure dates as recorded for different states

alternatively, it followed only the land route up Central America and through Mexico.

Prior to twenty years ago there was little evidence to show that birds actually crossed the Gulf of Mexico in any appreciable numbers, but evidence since has been cited to show that they not only take what is substantially a route across the eastern *edge* of the Gulf, that is, island hopping to Cuba and Florida, and also take the route around the western edge of the Gulf of Mexico, but spring and fall trans-Gulf migration in magnitude is now proven to the satisfaction of all modern naturalists and ornithologists.

It is reasonable to assume that many martins cross by island hopping (via Cuba to Florida), a supposition which is supported by the late fall departure from Florida of vast numbers of these birds. A similarly large number also migrate up the land mass of Central America and Mexico into the United States. These different routes, followed by various martin flocks, may well account for

GOURD CLOSE-UP

TYPICAL RURAL
GOURD COLONY

the variation of arrival dates in different states throughout the country.

There is ample evidence cited by prominent ornithologists showing incoming flights in spring on the northern Gulf coast that involve migrations of the highest possible magnitude. These flights take place day after day. Radar evidence and 16 mm time-lapse photography attest to the trans-Gulf migration of many species of birds, including the Purple Martin.

Lowery cites as further evidence of trans-Gulf migration his observation of Purple Martins arriving in spring from across the open waters of the Gulf, that is, making a landfall. Also, the photographs of birds on the S. S. *West Quechee,* when it was caught in the eye of a hurricane on August 25, 1926, at a point 125 miles south of the Louisiana coast, shows hundreds of Purple Martins lined up on the rails and rigging.

It is a known fact that migratory birds are sometimes blown from their course by a sudden change of

MARTIN TYPE
GOURDS GROWING
ON A WIRE FENCE

CLOSE COMMUNION

winds and are forced to land prematurely through exhaustion. If they are over water, there is nothing to do but surrender to the surging sea below. Biologists have on occasion found song birds in the stomachs of sharks, a pathetic verification of the dangers of trans-Gulf migration.

A Mobile, Alabama dentist, Dr. Gaillard, spends much of his spare time on Dauphin Island, just south of Mobile, ministering to the needs of thousands of birds of many species when they alight there in the course of their spring and fall migrations. Dauphin Island is a 164-acre tract of wooded area which has been officially designated as a bird sanctuary.

According to Dr. Gaillard, the spring migration flights seem more exhausting for the birds than those in the fall. Perhaps this is because a place like Dauphin Island, close to the mainland, is receiving birds that have just completed a long over-water flight across the Gulf, which, when associated with adverse winds, forced them to descend on the first land. However, in the face of favorable weather, birds do not often stop on the first land but instead sometimes fly far inland. This is the principle of the "coastal hiatus" about which much has been written in ornithological journals.

Dr. Odum at the University of Georgia, in his studies on the energy reserves of migrants has shown that except when faced with prolonged periods of adverse winds, migrants are capable of sustained flights covering distances much greater than the breadth of the Gulf of Mexico and the Caribbean combined.

Dr. Gaillard reports that during the spring migration he found it easy to net hundreds of birds too exhausted to resist capture. Upon examination he found that they had worked off practically all of the fat deposits normally stored. Ship captains sailing back and forth across the Gulf of Mexico have confirmed the fact that many birds have fallen into the Gulf when they were forced to use up their reserve energy or failed to build up a proper reserve before leaving.

Gaillard reports further that once he saw a flight of several hundred birds heading south over the island, into the Gulf. They quickly realized they had overshot the usual landing field and returned to feed and rest. He immediately bought up several thousands of crickets from nearby bait shops and fed them to the birds from beneath a wire fence which he had erected as a kind of mass-production bird feeder. After rest and refueling, this flock eventually continued on its way past Dauphin Island and out to sea on its annual southward migration to South America.

Land migration of martins, like some other birds, often takes place at relatively low altitudes (below 300 feet) and following the ground level, rising and falling with the terrain below. Across the water, too, at times they have been observed to fly at quite low altitudes, very near the surface of the water. A possible explanation for this low flight pattern is that this would serve to give some protection from strong winds that may be blowing in the opposite direction from their flight pattern. Also, it is this low flight pattern which makes them especially vulnerable to high land objects such as television towers, office, buildings, lighthouses, and so on, which lie in their lane of flight. One report tells of Purple Martins killed on a highway bridge over Albermarle Sound, North Carolina. Driving across the bridge, an observer noticed hundreds of dead birds, all Purple Martins. Since there were no dead birds along the road, only on the bridge, he concluded that the martins came to this fate by flying against the blinding headlights of automobiles as they came to roost on the railings of the bridge.

Later on the same bridge another passerby observed a large flock of Purple Martins circling down to roost on the supporting beams beneath the bridge (rather than the railings). A thunderstorm suddenly broke and the circling martins were forced lower and lower by the weather until they were so low that automobiles struck them. Only a few landed on the highway unharmed and all were drenched by the sudden cloudburst. The observer counted 173 martins on the bridge, of which 169 were dead, having been either crushed in the air or struck while on the roadway. Weather is often the deterrent factor for flight patterns and altitudes of the Purple Martin, whether across land or water.

An Amazing Circumstance

Lowery and assistants released eight banded male Purple Martins (from a roost in Baton Rouge) over the middle of the Gulf of Mexico to find out how long would be required for them to return to their nests in Baton Rouge. This, they calculated, would be an interesting observation to make on flight time of the Purple Martin, though admittedly no scientific investigation. Unfortunately, a cold front moved in before the return of the martins, and none of the eight birds showed up for several days.

When this happened, a local newspaper headlined the story, "WIVES OF MARTINS MOURN HUBBIES LOST AT SEA." In the end only three martins arrived safely that were accounted for. The remainder were presumed to have arrived safely in other parts, to wend their way home later. Because of the abnormal conditions under which the experiment concluded, no attempt was made to draw from it any conclusions at all about the Purple Martin. Instead, it furnished Dr. Lowery and his readers with an interesting though different piece of news for the day.

A RURAL INSTAL-
LATION

IN A CITY PARK

SOUTHERN DECOR

COMMERCIAL
DELIGHT

THE MARTIN HOUSE

Style and Size

Successful martin houses can vary from a simple gourd to the sophisticated multi-plex apartment. Imagination and taste are the only restrictions on the plan to be followed. Placed throughout this book are pictures that will provide the reader with a fairly comprehensive idea of the styles now being followed by martin enthusiasts, as well as the proper way to erect the houses.

Erect The House In Time

Whatever kind of bird house one uses, he should be prepared to *erect it just prior to the martins' arrival,* or as soon as he observes that the first birds (the males) have arrived. In such a way he may prevent sparrows and starlings from building before the martins arrive. For this purpose, it is important to use the map of arrival times to plan the erection date for your vicinity, and to perfect its data with your own yearly observations.

With good luck, this would-be martin fancier will attract martins to his bird house the first year he puts it out. An acquaintance of the writer had such luck: his new colony of martins "were so glad to see the house they could not wait until it was up. While it was being put up they flew around it, singing and fluttering about it, and when it was half-way up, they all lit upon it and rode up with it".

Not everyone may be so lucky the first time he tries. A perfectly fine martin house may be erected and yet not attract martins the first year or two. The United States is, after all, a large country and the little martin house is a very small and inconspicuous land mark at best. Indeed, it seems amazing that this little bird can find the house at all. Furthermore, from year to year, the martin usually returns to the same house in which it last lived, rather than seeking a new home.

It is from the martins' population explosion that the new colonies usually form. The younger birds are forced to find other nesting places than their home, and it is from this group, or from a colony dissatisfied for some reason or other with its old nesting site, that the new martin enthusiast will get his own colony of martins. There may be other reasons for the failure to attract martins the first year one tries. A sudden spring cold spell, with rains and chilling winds, may destroy many of these birds because it decimates their food supply of insects. Inclement weather has also been known to force martins southward from their usual path of flight in early spring before nesting has begun. Often they will not return in such a year. Many calamities can befall the flock as they journey to and from their Latin American sojourn. The writer knows of Purple Martin colonies which built regularly at their nesting sites and then for some mysterious reason skipped a year or two before returning. It is thus possible for the entire colony to be wiped out for a year or more. Only later do entirely new martins discover the house and establish themselves there.

Regretably, the increasing use of commercial insecticides has eradicated so many insects that martins must sometimes move away from an area that is too often sprayed, since there must be a large food supply for the martin to feed upon at all times. Insecticides have also known to have a detrimental effect upon the birds themselves.

In some cases martin enthusiasts have seen the first martins arrive, look over their bird houses and then move on for some unexplainable reason. This does not mean, however, that the house will not be occupied in subsequent seasons. There are in fact various reasons why this can happen. The martins may have alighted only in route to another site, never intending to establish a home there at all. Force of habit is very strong and martins habitually return to former nesting sites unless forced to leave

DELIGHTFUL TWENTY-PLEX

MARTIN COLONY VARIETY

125

SATISFACTION FOR
MANY

ALONG THE FREEWAY

because of crowding or unfavorable environment. (One ornithologist banded over 500 Purple Martins that all returned to their original nesting sites in the following year.) It is possible, too, to experiment with the exact location of one's bird house if no martins nest in it initially. The writer has known martin enthusiasts who found it necessary to relocate their houses before the birds would build. Erecting martin houses too late in the season can also result in failure to attract the birds; here, too, experimentation can be recommended. For certain, Purple Martins will not build in houses that are erected near trees. They insist upon an open area and have been known to leave houses that have had trees grow up too near them.

Martins perhaps are extremely aware of the local conditions around their nesting site and of any changes in the position of the bird house. A correspondent of the writer substantiates this with the story of his first year of martin raising. He built a large colony of bird houses made from gourds which he disassembled at the end of the season (quite properly), cleaned, sprayed for insects and stored for the winter. He replaced the gourds on March 2 of the year, just in time for the arrival of the birds, but in doing so, he erected the gourd houses in a random sequence, not being particular to place each in the location it had previously occupied. He related that "these were the most confused birds you could ever hope to see, and it took days for them to settle down to occupancy and nesting." From that time on, he was careful to number all gourds as they were taken down, and to replace them in the same order the following year. Thereafter the birds nested without complaint. It is perhaps well to take this gentleman's experience to heart when one decides to replace the bird house each year.

The House Itself

Martin houses can vary not only in size but also in height above the ground. And, of course, the birds will sometimes nest in other objects besides what is intended for them. Some years ago a martin family in Baton Rouge selected a most unorthodox nesting site, a rural mail box (only four feet above the ground) on the edge of the Louisiana State University campus.

This is not the usual case though, for martin houses do best high off the ground. A usual martin house is supported at the end of a pole, 15 to 20 feet above the ground. Many of these poles are hinged near the base so they can be lowered at the end of the season to facilitate cleaning of the box. This point is rather important, for regular cleaning out of the nests, abandoned for the season, helps to eradicate insects that might infest the apartments. It is well to spray the inside of the bird house with an insecticide after cleaning, and to store the house in the winter season.

The recommended measurements for each apartment in the bird house are 8 x 8 x 8 inches, with an entrance hole (preferably round) about 2 inches in

INDIVIDUAL SE-CURITY

A ROOFTOP INSTALLATION

diameter and 1 to 1½ inches above the floor of the apartment. Some fanciers prefer to place the holes close to the floor level because martins have short legs. Yet, a higher entrance hole poses no problem and is an added protection feature for eggs and young within.

It is unrealistic to make the individual apartment any smaller than 8 x 8 inches, even though this is sometimes recommended in bird manuals, for the Purple Martin is 7 to 8 inches long. It would seem a shame for a bird to find it necessary to "curl up" in order to brood upon its nest. There is no doubt that the bird will adapt itself to a smaller apartment if that is all which is available, but this could cause it to abandon the house after the season is over and select a better site the following year. Particularly is this true with the wide variety of homes being offered to him by man today. The proper height of a martin apartment is eight inches, also; though a variation of from 6 to 8 inches will do. The writer himself prefers to use houses with cubical apartments, 8" x 8" x 8". This size offers two

FOR THOSE WHO
PREFER QUANTITY

IN AN APARTMENT
HOUSE PATIO
SCENE

132

THIS ONE HAS
RAISED MANY

ACCOMMODATIONS
FOR MANY

A TYPICAL SCENE

JAPANESE MOTIF

advantages: the cubical shape adds simplicity to build the house, while the added height provides added ventilation space and thus reduces the summer heat inside the house.

A hollow gourd makes an attractive house and one which is well-liked by martins. The crooked neck of the gourd provides an easy perch for the martins and the curvature of the gourd itself provides a perch also when the hole is cut. On the other hand, martin houses built from scratch must be supplied with a porch. It is essential to the martins' ability to enter the apartment with ease - and also provides added amusement for human observers of the martins as they hop back and forth on the porch. A railing along the front of the porch will provide protection for the young by preventing them from falling from the porch before they are ready to fly. The porch should be at least three inches deep, for anything less will not provide sufficient room for the birds to move about with comfort while perched upon the railing.

The bird house should be placed in a fairly open

area, away from other tall objects from which predatory animals like cats and squirrels might jump, and affording ample room for flight around the roof of the house. The house should not be too near woods or other buildings. A martin house actually placed within a wooded area is likely never to be occupied.

If your bird house is placed near a pond, lake or stream, you will enjoy the added attraction of seeing the martins swoop down to drink on the wing. The young birds that have just begun to fly are taught this technique by the parent bird. Sometimes they will make two or three trial runs before finally reaching success (somewhat like a student aviator making his first landing attempt).

It is definitely established that martins will nest in more remote or primitive places, for martin nests are found in hollow trees, crevices in large buildings, holes in broken downspouts, and even atop a light pole and in open pipes. Their strong preference, however, is for houses constructed by man.

IN EARLY SPRING

STYLIZED

For example, a study of martin nesting was made in a given area of Kansas. In every instance the martins nested in artificially constructed houses. Most of these were painted white, had porches and were at least eight feet off the ground. All were in an open area and none was directly under a tree of any description. In fact, for the purpose of control, a hollow tree trunk twelve feet tall, having a natural cavity and an entrance hole high off the ground, was placed near one of the colonies to see if martins would nest in it as well. When they would not, the entrance hole was edged in white to elicit further attraction, but still to no avail.

As a boy of 10, this writer constructed his first martin house — from a wooden apple box, with a partition in the middle and four square openings in the sides. This house was erected on a long pole secured to a fence post with barbed wire. During the first season he raised martins, sparrows, bluebirds, all in the same box. Many battles ensued, but each of these species seemed to raise a brood

PINE TREE BACKGROUND

COMMERCIAL DELIGHT

of young birds successfully. Since that time, he has graduated to a more sophisticated house design, with nine to twelve apartments, and has usually succeeded in raising exclusively martins, with the exception of a sparrow or two.

The number of rooms in a martin house is entirely up to the owner who maintains it. It may range from two to thirty or forty apartments — even groups of hundreds of apartments have been erected by cooperative effort in various towns and cities across the country. If one does not care to design or build his own Purple Martin house, there are commercial houses where he can secure a ready-made house. These are often advertised in gift catalogues, monthly magazines, newspapers, and in the yard and garden stores. If he prefers to build his own, several tried and true plans are shown in photographs throughout this volume. Building your own house offers many possibilities for designs which cannot be found in the commercially available models. Certainly no one who is a woodworking

WITHIN EASY VIEW

TRIED AND TRUE

141

PATIO OFFERING

SPACIOUS
ORIENTATION

enthusiast should ever buy a martin house, for building the house can be an appreciably enjoyable part of the experience of martin fancying. Building one's own bird house also permits the builder to adapt its design to the decor of his own house and its environment. Besides, this is an excellent way to work with young son in a father-son relationship, so much needed today. It permits, too, off-season leisurely building during summer, fall, and winter months. A set of ten complete plans is available from the author (see listing at end of Bibliography).

It is important to have plugs for the entrance holes. These allow you to close the apartments while the martins are away and thus prevent sparrows and starlings from taking over in their absence. This is of especial value in instances where the house cannot be removed for cleaning each year. If at all possible, however, the house should be taken down for cleaning, repainting (when necessary) and stored for the winter.

An attractive arrangement of gourds will be

welcomed by the martin family and can be arranged to lend a charming atmosphere to the premises. One can purchase gourd seeds through advertisements in farm journals and newspapers.

When preparing the gourd, it is well to cut the entrance hole with a two-inch drill bit or circular saw fitted into the end of an electric drill. This insures a neatly cut hole and simplifies the work tremendously. Small drain holes must be bored into the bottom of each gourd to permit rain water to run out, otherwise the young birds run the risk of drowning. A one-fourth or one-half inch drill should be used for this and the small bulbous areas of the gourd are the proper locations for these holes. Unlike box-shaped houses, gourds should be swung from supporting cross arms rather than being secured by the neck of the gourd, since the martins seem to appreciate swinging houses. This feature can help prevent sparrows from building, for the sparrow oftentimes shuns a movable bird house.

One will notice that among the many gourd houses in the photograph there can be seen clorox jugs, also made

into bird houses. Some of these are white and some are blue, but none of the white ones were built in. The owner of this colony speculated that martins were reluctant to build in these owing to their almost transparancy, which permitted too much light to penetrate the sides. On the other hand, every blue jug contained a martin nest.

Perhaps some unique arrangement of jugs can be determined by the reader that would make them acceptable to the typical home environment. At least here is an unusual possibility for the martin house.

Television Antennas As Supports

In his observations of many modern colonies the writer has observed the many television aerials atop houses across the country, with almost every house, rich or poor, sporting a TV mast on the house. The thought immediately occurred that this TV mast is a natural martin house pole as well. Surely the two functions could be combined. Immediately upon return home from such a trip the author made a TV martin house and erected it for observation. As might be expected, the very first year martins took to this new house (shown on the following page). Attachment of the bird house does not interfere with television reception, and since the electric current does not flow through the antenna or mast, it is completely safe for martins. Furthermore, the bird house need not detract from the architectural tastefulness in such a case, indeed it can enhance it more than the bare pole of the TV mast alone. The writer recommends a balanced pair of vertical bird houses, as shown in the following picture.

BALANCED PAIR

Most of the TV antennas are deliberately erected for easy access from the roof top, certainly another advantage.

A few words of caution are necessary here. The martin house must be hung *above* the brace wires of the antenna (where such wires are used) to prevent the martins' flying into the wires. Since a martin never approaches the bird house from below, the house can be located immediately above the brace wires if necessary. On the other hand, it must be hung low enough on the pole so that the bars of the aerial above will not interfere with the bird's flight. The top of the aerial is likely to be a favorite perch for the colony of adult birds throughout the summer months (there is no possibility of this interfering with the television reception, however).

One's imagination alone will be the only limit upon the design for his martin houses if he follows the basic principles we have outlined above. Four TV houses could be swung from two cross arms at right angles. A series of gourds, too, would make a pleasing arrangement, particularly if painted different pastel colors in harmony with those of the residence below. A series of simple pulleys and cords can be used to lower martin houses from sites not easily reached from the housetop.

While martins are not easily disturbed by human beings, they have sometimes been known to build only on the side of the bird house farthest from human activity. One martin lover in Warrentown, Virginia located his martin house in such a place that dogs and children below disturbed the birds and found that the martins built on the far side only, away from the dogs and children at play. When he turned the house around so the martins could be seen from below, these birds immediately deserted their nests and rebuilt on the new far side. This is perhaps not the usual case, and under ordinary circumstances one need have little fear of distracting these birds. Many ornithologists have banded Purple Martins regularly without any disrupting of the martins' nesting. The mere passing of people on the lawns below the house certainly creates no distraction to the martins.

White painted houses, as previously referred to, have been found more to the liking of the Purple Martin than any other color and also reflect the heat better, an important factor. Ventilation holes near the top of each apartment are also assets, as well as drain holes in the floor to allow rain water to escape.

A MARTIN LOVER'S
DREAM

FOR SPACIOUS
GROUNDS

GENERAL HOUSE CONSTRUCTION TIPS

Your Purple Martin house may be erected on a wooden pole, 4" by 4", or a metal pipe (1½" in diameter). It is important to mount the house so that it may be lowered each year for cleaning and painting again. Nests should be removed each year after the season is over, best done with ice cube tongs, and then the house should be sprayed for insects. Repaint the house before storing for another season, or you might forget to do this.

We suggest using ¼" thick exterior-plywood for the martin house. This comes in 4' x 8' sheets and often a half-sheet can be bought at the lumber yard, if that is sufficient for the house which you plan to build.

Nails should be 1" wire nails with heads. A coping saw or a seven blade hole saw (fits into a ¼" drill) may be used to cut the entrance holes. All entrance holes should be 2" in diameter and bored 2¼" from the floor to the center of the hole. While not necessary, dowel rods for railings, ¼" diameter size, can be installed on the house to prevent the young from falling from the porch and also to provide a nice perch for the adults. Two drain holes (3/8" or ½" diameter) should be bored through the bottom of each apartment to let out any rain water that collects and also should be bored at the top of each apartment to permit ventilation. A pipe flange can be attached to the threaded end of the pipe (1½" diameter) for house attachment. Use flat head wood screws to fasten it to the house. Asphalt saturated building felt can be used for roofing and it can be painted the same color as the house. Two coats will prevent the asphalt from bleeding through. Tack the roofing on with small carpet tacks before painting.

For large houses it is well to attach a second piece of plywood to the bottom of the house to permit greater strength for the screws that attach the flange to the house. The house should be approximately 14' to 20' above the ground. This will not hold true if the house is mounted on top of the residence or the garage pole. Be sure, however, to mount the house high enough to prevent a stray cat from jumping up on it to get the young birds. Too, it is well to attach a 2' wide piece of tin around the pole if it is made of wood, about 7' or more above the ground level, to prevent a cat or squirrel from climbing the pole.

The house should be mounted in the open so that the birds may easily approach it in flight. Birds will not build in a house that does not provide an open approach. This fact is worth emphasizing again.

Shown in the following is a suggested mounting of the base of the pole to permit lowering each season to clean out the house, spray it for insects, and plug up the holes to prevent sparrows and starlings from using it until another martin season has arrived. If you save the round cut-outs when cutting your entrance holes, these can be used as plugs for the off-seasons by tacking a thin strip of wood (tongue depressers are good for this) across the front and on each side of the entrance hole to make it secure. Then upon arrival time for the Purple Martins, you merely

lower your house and remove these cover pieces, being
sure to save them until the next season. See the diagram
below.

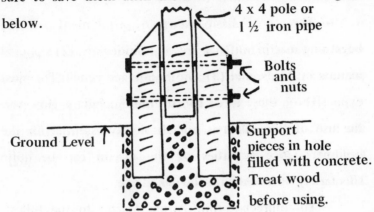

4 x 4 pole or
1 ½ iron pipe

Bolts
and
nuts

Ground Level

Support
pieces in hole
filled with concrete.
Treat wood
before using.

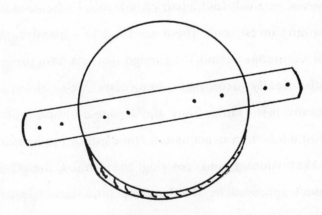

PLYWOOD PLUG

BINOCULARS – THE MARTIN WATCHER'S TOOL

The three basic items of equipment for the beginning martin watcher are: (1) binoculars, (2) a pocket manual on birds, and (3) a notebook and pencil. The most expensive of these is, of course, the binoculars. However, the use of binoculars is not absolutely essential for the beginner, since activities of the martin can be quite adequately observed with the naked eye.

To appreciate the Purple Martin to the fullest, however, one will find a pair of binoculars a tremendously rewarding investment. These need not be expensive, since both the domestic and the foreign markets have provided mechanically acceptable binoculars well within the economy price range. Since the Japanese optical industry has established an examination standard for products leaving that country and entering the United States, any product approved by the Japanese Importation Institute can be relied upon. Of course our domestic brands are excellent binoculars at various prices. Glasses of varying qualities can also be selected from the European market as well.

In selecting binoculars it is possible to buy too powerful an instrument. If this is done, one can find that it is almost impossible to hold the glass steady enough to see the bird, and he certainly will have difficulty following the martin in flight. Any glass more powerful than a 7 x 35 will prove to be unsatisfactory. The two most satisfactory sizes are 6 x 30 and 7 x 35; since the 6 x 30 size also is preferred for spectator sports, airplane watching, and for wooded areas, it is recommended here. In this terminology, "6" refers to the magnification power, that is, the number of times larger the image appears when seen through the lens, and "30" gives the size (in millimeters) of the diameter of the objective lenses (the objective lenses are the ones fartherest from the eye and closest to the view). The size of these lenses governs the light gathering capacity and thus the amount of light admitted into the binoculars. *Full coated lenses* are a valuable asset. Lens coating is a process invented during World War II to eliminate reflections from the lens and prevent the appearance of a slight haze within the binoculars.

In procuring binoculars, there is nearly always a choice of two focusing devices. These are called individual focusing *(I.F.)* and center focusing *(C.F.)*.

With the I.F. type, focusing is accomplished by turning *each* of the two eyepieces until the object can be seen best. Individual focus types are calibrated, that is, marked with a plus (+) or minus (−) for each eyepiece. One starts with each eyecap at 'zero' and then turns in the plus or minus direction until the best focus is obtained. Since there is a scale, the optimum focus may be noted and thus be set in advance the next time the binoculars are to be used. This is particularly valuable when different people use the same binoculars, and vary the positions. If only one person intends to use the binoculars, once he has set the eyepieces he can fasten them in place with scotch tape or electrician's tape. If one wishes to become a serious bird watcher, however, this type of glasses will not be convenient for short distances of 15 to 25 feet. Refocusing each eyepiece is slow and tedious, and by the time one has the binoculars set the bird will be gone.

The recommended type for bird watchers is thus the center focus type (C.F.). On these binoculars the left eye cap is always fixed and only the right eyecap is adjustable. Begin focusing by covering the right objective lens with the right palm as the glasses are held in viewing position and rotate the center focusing adjustment until the object is as clear as possible through the left barrel. Then reverse this procedure, covering the left eyepiece with the left hand and turning the right individual focus until the object can be seen distinctly. Note the setting of the right focus calibration. This type of binoculars offers the advantage of allowing the adjustment (right lens setting) needs to be made before each person uses the glasses, all necessary refocusing to follow the bird as it moves from one distance to another is accomplished merely by adjusting the center focus (not possible, of course, with I.F. glasses).

Most good field glasses have an indication of the "field of view" marked on them. This is the width of the area seen through the binoculars. Generally it is given in feet, such as "400 feet at 1000 yards." For some purposes (watching a football game or horse racing) the field of view is important, but for others, such as bird watching, it is not so, since the only object of interest is quite small. One cannot purchase a single instrument and expect it to be excellent for all purposes; however, the 6 x 30 and the 7 x 35 binoculars will be quite utilitarian and an ideal for martin watching.

Naturally the price of binoculars varies with the quality. For fifteen to twenty-five dollars one should be able to purchase a C.F. 6 x 30 with coated lenses and a leather carrying case.

BIRD BANDING — YES OR NO?

A serious bird watcher may sometimes become interested in more scientific study of birds. One possiblity is then *bird banding,* that is trapping birds (by specified harmless means) and attaching to their legs a tiny metal identification tag. This must not be done merely for amusement; indeed, there are legal restrictions on who can be a bird bander. There are certain qualifications which must be met; control of bird banding is in the hands of the United States Fish and Wildlife Service, which issues permits for bird banding. To be accepted one must not only meet the qualifications of the Service, but be willing to accept the outlined responsibilities for such scientific work. Once he has qualified and is issued a permit, he will be equipped with thin aluminum bands to put around birds' legs for identification. These birds will be marked with a serial number, such as "32-145689" or "A-569758"

A UNITED CAUSE (COURTESY YOUNG MENS
BUSINESS CLUB, LAKE CHARLES, LA.)

or "F and W Serv. Wash. D. C." These official bands and record forms are supplied the bird bander free of charge by the government.

Lately government policy regarding bird banding has become increasingly strict. A limited "moratorium" has been declared on the issuance of new bird banding permits. A definite need for ornithological information is required now for prospective banders rather than merely to be ready, willing, and able. New permits to qualified banders are issued as old permits are retired.

The Fish and Wildlife Service states that the "only justifiable purpose for placing a U. S. Fish and Wildlife Service band on a bird is the generation of scientifically usable data which accrues from that banding and/or the subsequent recovery of that bird." The laboratory states (1) that a person eligible for banding should be capable of, and prepared to submit legible, accurate, and complete records whenever requested, (2) that bandings must be for *quality* rather than *quantity*. Before placing a band on a bird, one should ask "Why am I banding this bird?" and whether the bird can be accurately *aged* and *sexed.* If not, then why band? Thus "banding with a purpose" is important.

The bird banding activities of the Fish and Wildlife Services laboratory are extensive. For example, in 1965, 2,715,143 bands were used and approximately 65,000 band recoveries were reported. Records were received on 1,731,809 birds banded, of which 465,744 were game species and 1,274,065 were non-game species. This work is so extensive that the Bird Banding Laboratory has been experiencing difficulties in coping with the volume of banding data produced each year.

Bander or not, if anyone should find a dead bird that has been banded, he should write the band number on a post card, stating where, how, and by whom the bird was found. This card can then be mailed to the Bird Banding Laboratory, Migratory Bird Population Station, Laurel, Maryland 20108. In return for such information he will

BARREL CROSS-SECTIONS
(COURTESY JIM ELLIS, HATTIESBURG, MISS.)

receive a reply stating the history of the bird that he found. All bird watchers, whether licensed banders or not, should be on the lookout for birds that have been banded. Skilled trappers of birds also lend their aid to bird study by reporting information found in their vicinity.

Bird banding studies have provided much scientific information about all birds and about Purple Martins in particular, their migration routes, their winter destination, whether they return to the same location, changes in population, destination of species, and much other important data. Bird banding, however, is not recommended for the average bird watcher, who probably would find the work itself tedious and less rewarding than observation for its own sake. Instead, be a bird watcher for the love of birds and the many enjoyable hours that they can provide. Study them for the pleasure they afford, and you will have a hobby that can prove unlimited in its possiblities for amusement.

FURTHER READING

Since this book is not written solely for ornithologists, I have not burdened the text with footnotes to locate the sources of the data which I have used. For readers who may wish to continue with more detailed reading on the Purple Martin, however, the following will be found of interest.

The most thorough and complete study perhaps is Robert W. Allen and Margaret M. Nice, *A Study of the Breeding Biology of the Purple Martin* (Notre Dame, 1952), which touches (in 60 pages) upon most of the topics I have mentioned in the preceeding chapters. It appeared as volume 47, number 3, of the *American Midland Naturalist.* The section on martins in A. C. Bent's *Life Histories of North American Flycatchers, Larks, Swallows, and Their Allies* (reprinted as a Dover paperback: New York, 1963) is also quite valuable though now out of date. The relevant chapter in George H. Lowery, Jr's

Louisiana Birds (Baton Rouge, 1955) is excellent.

Various studies of a more specialized nature have also been written.

FOOD: R. Johnston,"Seasonal Variations in the Food of the Purple Martin." in *IBIS,* 109 (1967) 8-13.

H. W. Kale II, "The Relationship of Purple Martins to Mosquito Control," *AUK* 80 (1968) 654-661.

LIVING HABITS: P. Traverner, "Purple Martins Gathering Leaves," *AUK* 50 (1933) 110-111; A. Gaunt, "Behavior in the Purple Martin," *Bulletin of the Kansas Ornithological Society,* 10 (December 1959) 14-16; M. Cater, "Roosting Habits of Martins at Tucson, Arizona, *CONDOR* 46 (1944) 15-18, very detailed; H. Oberholser, "Another Purple Martin Roost in the City of Washington," *BIRD-LORE,* 19, No. 6 (December 1917) 96-99; A. and A. Anderson, "Notes on the Purple Martin Roost at Tucson," *CONDOR,* 48 (1946), 15-18; G. Ziegler, "Notes on a Purple Martin Colony, *"AUK,* 40 (1923) 431-436.

COLOR: R. Johnston,"The Adaptive Basis of Geographic

Variation in Color of the Purple Martin," *CONDOR,* 68 (1966) 219-228.

HOMING AND MIGRATION: W. Southern, "Homing of Purple Martins," *WILSON BULLETIN,* 71 (1958) 254-261; G. Lowery and R. Newman, "Mysteries of Migration," in Alexander Wetmore, *Water, Prey, and Game Birds of North America* (National Geographic Society), excellent and very readable; Lowery and Newman, "A Continental View of Bird Migration on Four Nights in October," *AUK* 83 (1966) 547-586; Dorst, Jean, *The Migration of Birds* (Boston) 1962, excellent on migration.

MORTALITY: N. Hill, "Purple Martins Killed on a Bridge," *AUK* 65 (1948) 448-449; M. Jacobson, "Purple Martins Killed on a Highway," *AUK* (1947) 64, 456-457; Horton, F., "Mortality of Purple Martins at Brattleboro, Vermont," *AUK* 20 (1903) 435-436. Other technical studies are cited in Alice and Nice, Study of the Breeding Biology . . . (above) and the other books and articles just mentioned. A useful field guide to the birds of North America is Chandler S. Robbins; Bruun, Bertel; and Zim, Herbert S., *Guide to Field Identification — Birds of North America* (New York, 1966). For general introductory reading to accompany this, there are several recent books including Joel C. Welty, *The Life of Birds* (New York, 1963), good on biology and migration; and Leonard Wing, *Natural History of Birds* (New York, 1956), companion to a field guide. Finally, I will mention the Purple Martin newspaper published by the Trio Manufacturing Company, Griggsville, Illinois (a commercial producer of birds houses), which is called the *Purple Martin Capitol News.* The *News* has been published since 1966, with the admirable aim of promoting general interest in the Purple Martin, and while it is not a scholarly publication, the pictures and articles are usually quite interesting.

PARTIAL BIBLIOGRAPHY

Allen, Robert W. and Nice, Margaret M. 1952. *A Study of the Breeding Biology of the Purple Martin.* The University of Notre Dame Press, Notre Dame, Indiana.

American Ornithologists' Union. 1957. *Check-list of North American Birds.* Lord Baltimore Press, Baltimore, Maryland.

Anderson, A. H. and Anderson, Anne. 1948. " Notes on the Purple Martin Roost at Tucson," Condor, 48: 140-141.

Beal, F. E. L. 1918. "Food Habits of the Swallows, a Family of Valuable Native Birds," United States Department of Agriculture Bulletin No. 619.

Bent, Arthur Cleveland. 1963. *Life History of North*

American Flycatchers, Larks, Swallows, and Their Allies. Dover Publications, New York.

Blake, C. E. 1947. "Wing Flapping Rate of Birds," Auk, 64:619-620.

_____ 1948. "The Flight of Swallows," 65: 54-62.

Burleigh, Thomas D. 1941. *Georgia Birds.* Georgia Ornithological Society, Atlanta, Georgia.

Cater, Milam B. 1944. "Roosting Habits of Martins at Tucson, Arizona," Condor, 46: 15-18.

Chapman, Frank M. 1932. *Handbook of Birds of Eastern North America.* Appleton Century, New York.

de Schauensee, Rodolphe Meyer. 1966. *The Species of*

Birds of South America and Their Distribution. Academy of Natural Sciences of Philadelphia Pennsylvania.

_____ 1964. *Birds of Colombia.* Livingston Publishing Company, Wynnewood. Pennyslvania.

Dorst, Jean. 1962. *The Migration of Birds.* Houghton Mifflin Company, Boston, Massachusetts.

Forbush, Edward Howe. 1929. *Birds of Massachusetts and Other New England States,* Volume 3.

Ford, Alice. 1957. *Bird Biographies of James J. Audubon.* The Macmillan Company, New York.

Gabrielson, I. N. and Lincoln, Frederick C. *Birds of Alaska.* Stockpole Company, Harrisburg, Pennsylvania and Wildlife Management Institute, Washington, D. C.

Gaunt, Abbot S. 1959. *Bulletin,* Kansas Ornithological Society, 10:14-16.

_____ 1923. "Birds of the New York Region," American Museum of Natural History, Handbook Series, No. 9, United States Printing Office, Washington, D. C.

Griffin, Donald R. 1964. "Bird Migration," Natural History Press, Garden City, New York.

Griscom, L. 1941. "Audubon Magazine," 43:191-196.

Hill, N. P. 1948. "Purple Martins Killed on a Bridge," Auk, 65: 448-449.

Horton, Frances B. 1903. "Mortality of Purple Martins at Brattleboro, Vermont," Auk, 20: 435-436.

Imhoff, Thomas A. 1962. *Alabama Birds.* University of Alabama Press, Tuscaloosa, Alabama.

Johnston, Richard F. 1966. "The Adaptive Basis of Geographic Variation in Color of the Purple Martin," Cooper Ornithological Society, 68: 219-228.

_____ "Seasonal Variation in the Food of the Purple Martin," Ibis, 109: 8-13.

Kale, Herbert W. II. 1968. "The Relationship of Purple Martins to Mosquito Control, " Auk, *85*: 654- 66l.

Lincoln, Frederick C. 1950. *Migration of Birds.* United States Department of the Interior, Fish and Wildlife Service, Circular No. 16.

Lowery, George H. Jr. 1955. *Louisiana Birds.* Louisiana State University Press, Baton Rouge, Louisiana.

_____ and Newman, Robert J. "A Continent-wide View of Bird Migration on Four Nights in

October," Auk, 83: 547-586.

Mayr, Ernst and Greenway, James C. 1960. *Check-list of Birds of the World.* Volume 9, Museum of Comparative Zoology, Cambridge, Massachusetts.

Macnamara, Charles. 1917. "The Purple Martin," Ottawa National, 31: 49-54.

Mirchell, R. T. and Blagbrough, H. P. 1953. "The Effects of DDT Upon Survival and Growth of Nesting Songbirds," Journal of Wildlife Management, 17: 45-54.

Musselman, T. E. 1966. "T. E. Talks About Birds," Purple Martin Capitol News, Griggsville, Illinois, Vol. 1, page 3.

Oberholser, Harry C. "Another Purple Martin Roost in the

City of Washington," Bird-Lore, Volume 19, No. 6, Dec. 1917.

Robbins, Chandler S. and Bruun, Bertel and Zim, Herbert S. 1966. *Guide to Field Identification, Birds of North America.* Golden Press, New York.

Salvia, Osbert, and Godman, Frederick Duncane. *Biologia Centrali-Americana,* Volume 1.

Southern, W. E. "Homing of Purple Martins," Wilson Bulletin, 71: 254-261.

Southern Living, "Paradise of Songbirds," 2:20-21.

Sprunt, J. Alexander. 1954. *Florida Bird Life.* Coward-McCann, Inc. New York.

Taverner, Percy Algernon. 1933. "Purple Martins

Gathering Leaves," Auk, 50: 110-111.

Wade, J. L. 1966. *What You Should Know About the Purple Martin,* Griggsville, Illinois.

Wallace, George J. 1955. *An Introduction to Ornithology.* Macmillan Company, New York.

Widmann, Otto. 1884. "How Young Martins Are Fed,"Field and Stream, 22:484.

Welty, Joel C. 1963. *The Life of Birds.* Alfred C. Knopf, New York.

Wetmore, Alexander. 1965. *Water, Prey, and , Game Birds of North America.* National Geographic Society, Washington, D. C.

Williams, George G. 1950. "The Nature and Causes of the

'Coastal Hiatus'," Wilson Bulletin, 62: 175-182.

_____ 1951, "Birds Against the Moon," *Nature Notes from the Gulf States* (winter) 1951.

_____ 1952, "Birds on the Gulf of Mexico," Auk, 69: 428-431.

Wing, Leonard C. 1956. *Natural History of Birds.* Ronald Press, New York.

Ziegler, George Frederick, Jr. "Notes on the Purple Martin Colony," Auk, 40: 431-436.

PERSONAL OBSERVATIONS

Date of arrival	M	F	Time of day	Weather T° con.		Nest building starts	Adults observed M	F	No. Apts. occupied	First young heard
Example: 2-28-69 3-1-69	✓	✓	7:05 a.m.	40	fair	3-15-69	3	3	8	4-5-69

PERSONAL OBSERVATIONS

Young in each apartment	Young's first flight	Colony departs	NOTES
	4-30-69	6-1-69	one apartment was not occupied this year.

PERSONAL OBSERVATIONS

Date of arrival	M	F	Time of day	Weather T° con.	Nest building starts	Adults observed M	F	No. apts. occupied	First young heard

PERSONAL OBSERVATIONS

Young in each apartment	Young's first flight	Colony departs	NOTES

PERSONAL OBSERVATIONS

Date of arrival	M	F	Time of day	Weather T°	Cond -ition	Nest building starts	Adults observed M	F	No. Apts. occupied	First young heard

PERSONAL OBSERVATIONS

Young in each apartment	Young's first flight	Colony departs	NOTES

PERSONAL OBSERVATIONS

Date of arrival	M	F	Time of day	Weather T°	cond	Nest building starts	Adults observed M	F	No. Apts. occupied	First young heard

PERSONAL OBSERVATIONS

Young in in each apartment	Young's first flight	Colony departs	

OBSERVATIONS OF OTHERS

OBSERVATIONS OF OTHERS

will not build in box

KINGBIRD

long forked tail

BARN
SWALLOW

CLIFF

SWALLOW

will not build in box

an immediate interloper

STARLING
the only black bird (adult)

with a yellow bill

HOUSE
SPARROW

will build
in box

an immediate interloper

FLY-
CATCHER

CHIMNEY
SWIFT

always flying   cigar-shaped body

SILOUETTES OF BIRDS OFTEN

PURPLE GRACKLE

longer tail, straight flight

COWBIRD

long boat tail

BOAT-TAILED GRACKLE

brown head

MISTAKEN FOR THE PURPLE MARTIN